Self Talk,

Think Like A Child

Author: R Dean Akers

ISBN-13: 9781642540482

Dedication

This book is dedicated to:

My 5 Sons, Wife and Dad.

My 5 sons inspired me every day while they grew up to look at life through the simple eyes of a child. While they're older now, I get to experience this same exciting reminder with my grandchildren.

My wife, Michelle who always has my back and supports me in my quest to eliminate self-talk around me and build our life full of successes and fun.

My Dad who always encouraged me to never assume anything and look for all the possibilities in everything. Look for the facts and not what is said.

This is also dedicated to all the Entrepreneurs that didn't listen to all of their naysayers and pushed on to create businesses, products and evolutionary changes in our world.

I hope this book helps or inspires at least one person to think like a child and eliminate their own self talk

About the Author

Dean has mastered the art form of seizing opportunities in any situation. As a University of Florida graduate, he joined a company in Lakeland Florida as a warehouse runner. By the age of 28 he was made the Vice President of Sales. It was during the recession of the 80's. Under the philosophies he will share with us today he was able to take this organization from 50 million in sales to 103 million 2 years later. This was done with the same 300 folks that did 50 million.

At 30 he wanted his own business, so he bought a chain of tire stores. This became a fix it program. He grew it from a financially broke company to the leading commercial tire company in the state of Florida. He sold it to Don Olson tire and retired at age 40.

His passion for helping others created his platform for Adjunct CEO. In this platform he has been helping others over the last 26 years.

His many companies he has owned and or directly helped have had been big successes in sales and profits.

The combined increase in sales of companies he's helped has been over 500 million dollars. His journey has been built on the foundation of Eliminating self-talk and thinking like a child

Table of Contents

Chapter 1

What Is "Thinking Like a Child?"

When a child is born, their mind is unpolluted and untouched by human conventions and beliefs. They look at the world without a filter and are eager to discover the new ways of this world. Innocence is abundant and curiosity at its peak. We often find children looking at a shadow and trying to chase it or looking at their own reflection with absolute wonder, talking to themselves. They draw strange figures or a scenery in which the sun is painted purple or green and the grass is blue. They go around the house painting on the walls or tables as if every other thing is a canvas for their creativity. They color outside of the lines, write stories that make no sense even sometimes make a beautiful work of fiction. They have wild imaginations with no boundaries. They are unafraid to make mistakes and are open to new adventures. This is what *'thinking like a child'* truly means.

Children have minds that have not been molded yet and therefore, their imagination expands beyond the horizon. There are no set limits and no boundaries for their thoughts. Although a child sees the same world that we look at, but their way of viewing everything is highly different from what an adult may have. As they grow older, their thoughts get influenced by the world. They begin to form opinions influenced by a set of rules instilled into their mind by the society.

Where the Influence Begins

The primary institution for a child is their family before they step out into the world. The family plays a vital part in teaching the child how to carry out basic tasks in their everyday life. It has been reported that a child asks about 300 questions in a day, which may even vary with their age. A child may bombard their family members with numerous questions regarding things that boggle their minds. They question the simplest things like why is the sky blue? Why is the moon visible during the day sometimes? What does a certain button do? Why do we die? Why do we go to school? How are babies born? Why do some people kill other people? Etc. While some questions like "How are babies born" may cause hesitation for the parents, and some may remain unanswered, there may be questions such as "Why do we go to school?" or "Why do some people kill other people?" that will incorporate an opinion in the minds of the children. They may no longer try to figure out the real reason and base their opinion on what they are fed.

For example, a child may be asked by their parents not to touch fire as they can get burned. This may arouse their curiosity and in return, they may end up trying to touch the fire with tiny hands only to find out how dangerous it is. This may instill a level of trust into their hearts for their parents and cause them to trust them in other situations without necessarily having to validate it. Similar things that are ingrained in a child and may be highly transforming for their personalities are religious or cultural beliefs, or sometimes even political ideas. They grow up believing that what they have been taught is true. This thought process may stick closely to them for the rest of their lives, not only being a foundation for their identity and actions but also affecting the people around them.

Development of Biasness

As a child grows up, how their questions are answered by the people around them and what they are taught transform their minds. The way these questions are answered, and curiosities are satisfied contributes significantly to a child's personality and outlook on life as they grow up. As a child grows older and their personality begins to take shape, it gives rise to bitterness and animosity. Truth is that not every single person you meet is similar to you – both in terms of personality and demeanor. When people of different caliber, background, and temperament come together, personality clashes are inevitable. Regardless of how easygoing and amicable you are, there will always be people you hold animosity for. And this animosity creates *biasness.*

To be *biased* means 'to have a strong inclination of the mind or a preconceived opinion about something or someone.' Although having a preconceived notion about a certain thing makes you more alert and focused but it also creates a mindset that is settled in one place and does not think out of the box. It regulates the flow of thoughts in one direction and blocks the creativity. We tend to base our thoughts on educational teachings, cultural beliefs, societal norms, etc. As a consequence, we become more careful about the choices we make, we become afraid of making mistakes to avoid criticism, we tend to brush off unique ideas, considering them to be absurd, and we end up sticking to a monotony which results in lack of innovation. Biasness may even minimize our capacity to think and make us resistant to any opposing ideas – and that is not good for your business.

Importance of Innovation in Business

Innovation is extremely pivotal to the expansion and success of a business. In the current age, businesses that exhibit or promote innovation are highly valued and prosperous. They encourage new ideas and incorporate efficient ways in their business strategies which attract customers, causing their business to thrive.

Innovation involves coming up with ideas without conforming to the mundane, general strategies. It creates a change that transforms the business, increasing its management, sustainability, and profitability. This may cause them to engage on an organizational level, increasing competitiveness and growth, making the world a better place and securing the future of the people. Nowadays, while innovation is given so much significance in not only the field of business or marketing but also in many other areas of life, the question arises "How do we achieve this innovation?"

How Thinking Like a Child Eliminates Biasness and Promotes Innovation

There are numerous characteristics of a child that we all need to learn from. We all have been a child at some point, but somehow, we lost the luster along the way to adulthood. Our minds have got entangled in the cares of this world and have been molded to think according to the stereotypical beliefs taught to us. As maturity creeps in, so does bitterness and animosity, placing a filter on our eyes through which we now view the world.

Innovation calls for a dire need for 'thinking like a child.' There is no other way through which innovation can be achieved. It stems from child-like thoughts and expands like a tree grows spreading its stems and bearing fruit, into a creative mind that not only thinks imaginatively but also gives birth to more creative and productive work.

Thinking like a child involves multiple characteristics that our minds have surprisingly disposed of. The predominant feature which a child's mind is comprised of is *curiosity*. It is defined as 'a strong desire to know or learn something.' It has given birth to millions of inventions and discoveries that have now made our lives easier. Imagine a life without electricity if Benjamin Franklin had not had the curiosity to discover electricity. If Thomas Edison had not invented the light bulb, our life would have been deprived of this discovery and we would have been in darkness, quite literally. What if Sir Isaac Newton would not have been so curious when the apple fell on his head? Gravity would not have been discovered. Imagine the loss with the lack of curiosity in the minds of these great revolutionaries. Lack of curiosity would have kept us ignorant of such amazing inventions and discoveries and our lives would have been really dull.

It is a tragic fact that curiosity is now on the brink of extinction. Curious thinkers may be considered crazy. History is filled with great people who were curious thinkers and wanted to do something no one dared to do. At some point, they must have had to experience criticism and one must always be prepared to be attacked with criticism when they take a step toward innovation.

The road to success in a business through innovation that requires 'thinking like a child' is not easy. Take Christopher Columbus for example. His curiosity led him to travel. People thought that he would not return but he did and in addition to that, he found out that the earth was not flat but round. Similarly, Albert Einstein challenged his own ideas to create laws of physics. Leonardo Di Vinci was a painter, writer, inventor, and mathematician. His curiosity led him to do so many things. There are numerous examples of people like Steve Jobs, Walt Disney, Isaac Newton, etc. The only common thing in these revolutionary personalities was curiosity. Curiosity involves a passion that perseveres and refuses to be stopped. This same unstoppable, child-like curiosity is required in the field of business. As a business entrepreneur, you learn to pursue your ambitions and set your goals in a place where though it may seem hard to be reached, there are realms of possibilities for success. Furthermore, curiosity eliminates all biasness and our natural capabilities of adapting to the rules of the world and promotes innovation.

Fixed Mindsets and the Need for Transformation

Media has played a huge role in keeping our minds transfixed on the things they project by presenting repetitive ideas as if to brainwash our minds. It is slowly planting ideas like seeds in the minds of people and twisting their thoughts to adapt to their own. These thoughts may be about political, economic, or religious beliefs or even artistic ideas. It sets a standard of what is trending, what must be given importance, what should be adopted in our personal lives, etc.

While media is a powerful influencer and spreads its roots worldwide with every passing day, education plays a significant role too. It sets a pattern that we follow gradually when we are growing up. Education gives us a direction to walk. It is passed down from generation to generation. It is like a confined space which cannot be escaped now as it has taken roots in our society.

While education still remains important, it is undeniable that it takes away the curiosity that is inherent in humans. It takes away the ability to look at things in a whole new dimension. These fixed mindsets also diminish the ability of self-discovery and may cause us difficulty in self-expression. This must be rectified and the use of one's own imagination should be promoted. We should learn to distinguish between what must be adopted and what must not be that is taught to us. We must take a clear look at the facts and transform our minds into what they used to be before they got polluted by the worldly ideas. Facts are necessary for us so that we may have a sense of direction.

A famous story from the Bible teaches us how curiosity has always been in human beings. Take a look at the story of Adam and Eve. God strongly advised Adam and Eve not to have the fruit from the tree of knowledge. However, curiosity jumped up inside of them when the serpent asked both of them to eat the fruit. And to taste the fruit, they ate it. While this may be a bad example of curiosity, teaching how curiosity can lead to harm, the only purpose to share this story is to point out the fact that curiosity is inherent in our nature.

Curiosity is very prominent in the behavior of artists. An artist thinks like a child. Pablo Picasso once said:

"Every child is an artist. The problem is how to remain an artist after he grows up."

He, being one of the greatest artists of his time, recognized how imperative it is to think like a child. If we take a look at his paintings, we get a glimpse into his mind as well. How he views the world and how he paints it down on his canvas is beautifully unique. People may find it difficult to perceive and interpret his paintings. His perspective was entirely different from an average person because he thought like a child. Similarly, there are thousands of examples of how curiosity gives birth to innovation.

When you think like a child, creativity flows out of you. You become open to ideas. You want to think beyond the set limits. You want to look for new possibilities. You refuse to have a fixed pattern for things. You ignore the negatives and focus on the positives. You climb up the ladders of success without thinking what the outcome could be. You think out of the box and paint outside of the lines. You let the lives of people be transformed by inspiring them just as you transform your own life.

Stimulating Creativity in the Business Environment

Business is a field that demands a lot of focus and presence of mind, but it also asks for creativity, as we have earlier talked about the need for innovation. All the while, we have been looking at other things that put filters in our minds and transform our child-like thinking. Let us take a look at how we are the ones who put filters on the minds of the people around us. They might be the ones who are working in our company or may even be a part of our team. We impact on their thought processes, intentionally or unintentionally through what we do. Whether it is management, business ownership, team leadership, marketing, or other roles in the business setting, there is a possibility that we keep repeating the old ideas and fail to encourage creativity and the use of imagination in the people around us. This may be due to the rise of competition that we choose to resist change.

We fear to take the leap of faith and to dive deep into ideas. We fear to risk our businesses and therefore, we choose to follow what is generally done all around the world.

Here are ways in which we can stimulate creativity in the business:

1. **Make use of advanced technology and the use of the internet:**
   Always take full advantage of technology and the internet to seek ideas to form strategies. Look at what other innovators did to transform their businesses. The Internet is a whole universe filled with a vast array of unique ideas of anything you may be looking for. You can look for inspiration from people on social networking sites and have one-to-one conversations with people who belong to the same field as you do.
   Make full use of technology and create new things.

2. **Change trends and dynamics in your workplace:**
   Instead of sticking to old ways that your company formerly operated in, try adopting new trends and dynamics to attract customers and make work interesting and attractive. Incorporate ideas that relate to the current trends around the world, so that the people may be excited to see your product. Changing dynamics may bring about a positive attitude in the customers and the employees may also develop an interest in work. Ask your employees for ideas so that they may feel heard and appreciated.

3. **Aim at responding to the expectations of your customers:**
   Try to respond to what customers expect from your business. Playing blind and ignorant of their needs and expectations would only result in a loss. Keep in mind that even though you are aiming for your own profit, you are still working on a larger scale which is impacting on so many people. Their opinion and demands definitely

need to be given importance. Keep in mind that a successful business always keeps their customers' views as their top priority.

4. **Think out of the box:**
   Introduce new ideas that are not generally given much thought. Think like a child when creating an artwork. Expand your mind by looking beyond what is expected of you.

5. **Collaborate:**
   Collaborate with people around you, or with other businesses. Two people with different perspectives may come up with a whole new idea that may attract the customers of both the businesses, resulting in a bigger profit. Create a bond with other organizations and join hands with other innovative thinkers. Creativity attracts creativity.

6. **Pay attention to complaints and take criticism positively:**
   Every business strategy which is different and is newly introduced may receive criticism. It is a blessing because it helps you understand your mistakes. However, like a child, you need to keep the negativity aside and just give it a go. Do not fear what people may say about your ideas. Just put it forward and watch it do wonders.

Thinking like a child does not mean that you have to think immaturely. It surely means to embrace the creative side of you. The side which rebels against the natural laws and seeks to break the rules, the side which runs across the pathway of ideas without once considering it absurd. Albert Einstein once said:

> *"If at first the idea is not absurd, then there is no hope for it."*

Absurd ideas give uniqueness. They have their own touch of madness and originality. Copying someone's ideas is not something a child does, and neither is it something that is appreciated or valued. Think differently from others but do not forget to share that uniqueness.

Think of it this way. In a world of monotony, what part can you play in causing a shift in the dynamics? What change would you like to make? Introduce a new idea, change the trends, embrace uniqueness, and try new things. Give your business a new touch of innovation by discarding old, dull ways that formerly designed your strategies. Take off the shell that is placed on you by media, education, economic, political, or religious beliefs. Explore your inner capabilities and suspend all judgments of yourself. Have the same playfulness of a child, look at things with the same wonder in your eyes, let out your inquisitiveness, and convert your inner reality into external reality. The world needs to be blessed with a mind like you. You just have to believe in your abilities and sail across the ocean of ideas like Christopher Columbus. For that, you need to strengthen your perspective that is shaped by your beliefs and values.

Chapter 2

How We Think Like We Do Today vs. Yesterday

Over the course of our lives, we experience various shifts in our thought processes. We get influenced by our families, educational and religious institutions or similar external forces that aim at sculpting, if not completely transforming, our characters, temperaments and thoughts. Then, we accumulate those teachings and values, which overtime develops into a bias mindset: racial, religious or gender based. We tend to view the world with the filter provided by fail to look at things with our own perspectives. Consequently, we lose our originality and a child-like ability of thinking. The uniqueness that we were once born with fades away, and we are forced to adapt to the worldly beliefs, customs and traditions.

In the previous chapter, we learned about "what is thinking like a child?" and the significance of curiosity in adapting to that mindset. Also, we got an overview about fixed mindsets and development of biasness. In this chapter, we will dive deeper into the creational process of our thoughts, the forces that influence them and our experiences. We would compare today's mindsets with the old and traditional mindsets of the people. It is imperative to learn how these things work, and what can be done to inspire people to embrace the new way of thinking i.e. thinking like a child.

The Origin of Core Beliefs

"Core Beliefs" are the fundamental beliefs that we have regarding the way we view ourselves, others, the world, and the future. These are the beliefs that are ingrained in us at the time of our childhood. They also develop overtime, and through significant experiences in our lives. If untreated, these core beliefs can take deep roots in our minds and turn into rigid thoughts, which are difficult to change. They can also make us blind to the truth and we may end up supporting these core beliefs, even when there is sufficient evidence available that contradicts its validity.

These core beliefs can therefore, make your thinking capacity narrower and you fail to look at things from a broader perspective. Curiosity dampens, and you rely on the already embedded information in your brain. There is lack of neutrality and acceptance of new ideas and perceptions. As a result, reshaping or reconstructing these beliefs can become close to impossible, and preconceived notions may be dominant choices or decisions. People may become reluctant to let go of them, which causes them to dwell on their narrow-minded beliefs.

Therefore, it is vital that we may identify these core beliefs before they aggravate into strong, unshakable ideologies. It is a kind of self-reflection or analysis of our own thinking process. Asking yourself questions like,

"Why is this so?", "Is it true?", "What impact can it have?" and *"Does it truly reflect my way of thinking?"* can truly enable you to barge through the door of core beliefs and think profoundly like a child

Difference Between How We Think Today & How We Used To Think

If we compare our new ways of thinking to how we used to think earlier, we may see a drastic change in the process. Although the changes are gradual, they may serve as a foundation for a lot of beliefs that we may not be aware of. Every single day our brain receives new information, and we accumulate them inside ourselves. Inelastic thoughts can leave little room for curiosity and imaginative thinking.

Back in the day, when we were children, our minds were unbiased and unaffected by the society's norms and values. We lived a care-free life with our thoughts flowing without a halt. We questioned things and their validity. We were always eager to learn new things. This is the mindset of an average young child. However, if it is contrasted to what we think in today's age, we do realize that we have become very confined in our own mental realms. We are unwilling to step out of our comfort zones, which leads to sticking with old beliefs which have been passed down to us.

Education, religion and societal values have carved our brains into a shape that reflects its beliefs accurately. We have forgotten our childishness, and we are forced to deal with things only the adult way. These core beliefs must be transformed, to create a better and more creative thought process. As a result, this creativity will enable us to attain a successful and prosperous future.

Challenging the Core Beliefs

Once you are done evaluating and identifying your core beliefs, challenge them by sticking to the "thinking like a child" principle. Think in a more objective manner rather than in a subjective one, as subjective thinking stems from those thoughts that are instilled in us by others. Embrace your curiosity basing them on facts, and then dissecting those facts by tallying them against each other. This can make us clear and successful thinkers, devoid of assumptions and preconceived notions.

This process of challenging the core beliefs is like a war against yourself as you aim to strip yourself of your former thinking, which has been polluted by the world. It is an act of carefully sifting through the layers of thoughts and removing the ones that are solely based on what your mind has been fed over the years. Therefore, it clearly is not an easy task. However, with much assistance and willingness to embrace the new paths of innovation, you can get rid of the dull layer of filter that is hindering you from touching the horizons of your abilities.

The first question that you do need to ask yourself *is "What are your convictions?"* This means that, is there something that you follow blindly without analyzing it and affirming it in the light of evidence.

We need to demolish these core beliefs if they are stopping us from looking at the world from a creative perspective. When you first recognize your incapability to see things clearly, you learn to make room for change. You start shifting your perspective, and then keep yourself in someone else's shoes to look at things from a different standpoint.

Although, it is highly significant to get rid of these core beliefs, it is obvious that new beliefs will be formed. Nevertheless, we must remember our true selves within this self-discovery

Bias Build-Up Resulting in Prominence of Self-Talk

Self-talk is your inner voice talking back to you. This is based and altered on your core beliefs or underlying thoughts that are actually not your own but founded on what has been taught to you. While we talk about eliminating this altered self-talk, it becomes important to start eliminating the biasness in the first place. Biasness that builds up over the years may result in self-talk which is a reflection of these core beliefs. It is a kind of internal chatter that helps you reason and make judgments. It causes negativity and makes you self-delusional.

Furthermore, it makes you less creative by stopping you from making extra efforts. Therefore, it is very important to dispose your mind of all biasness, so that you can stop self-talk from affecting you. Eliminating this altered self-talk can give you a new outlook on life and can help you think like a child. Your mind only speaks what's been buried inside, which is a result of what you have learned. Positivity and creativity can help you restructure your thinking and create constructive self-talk that aims towards your own welfare.

As we learned in the previous chapter, curiosity has been the one common thing in great thinkers, and so is constructive self-talk. A creative person knows how to deny what the mind constantly tells him to do, and he knows how to cling to what is creative and beneficial, both for him and for others.

The Legacy Habit

Legacy, as we all know, is something that has been passed down to us. It may include cultural values, beliefs, customs, ideas, thoughts, and traditions. It may originate from a place where we are not even aware, and we only accept it because it is taught to us since childhood. Legacy is all that we have to leave behind when we die. However, people may tend to leave something as a legacy that is not even based on facts. They just teach their children, and their children pass down their teachings to their own children. This ends up being a chain of thoughts that are not even analyzed before being transferred to others.

This is quite evident in business settings where organizations are totally unaware of their purpose and goals. The people working in such companies may only believe or do what their leader tells them to do. We can test this ourselves by asking a person belonging to a company about their aims. You can ask them, what are they aiming for? To which they are likely to reply that they have no idea about it.

This is the legacy habit that we all have acquired intentionally or unintentionally. We refuse to invest our time and thoughts in anything that requires going an extra mile. We don't analyze things from our own perspectives, and only rely on what others tell us to do. This is a lazy approach to life and may cause us to stay within the boundaries which handicaps us to explore our capabilities.

Analyzing Your Business

The questions that arise are, *"Does your business have a legacy habit?"*, *"Is it an innovative, creative business that builds up positivity and opens up new doors of possibilities?"* or *"Is it something that is passed down to you to carry on the legacy of other people?"*

It is vital that you analyze your business goals to have a better understanding of what you are promoting. If you are not aware of your own business policies, it will only hinder you from making important choices and decisions for the sole benefit of your company.

Evaluating your business goals will also ensure that you represent your company in the best possible way, not just to your customers but to your own employees. You have the ability to bring about a change that can be the new legacy to be carried on. And what's the best way than to go back to your childish ways and make creativity your priority.

Developing A Strategy to Eliminate the Legacy Habit

The legacy habit has become such a common practice in business that it stops companies from adapting to new, beneficial business strategies. People stick to old conventional ways and fail to achieve success in their businesses. They may fail to see the cause of this inability and may blame external forces or the low productivity of their own employees. They may not go to the core to find out the real reasons behind their financial backwardness. It's their own habits which are ingrained in them that hinder them in distinguishing the root cause.

Therefore, it is important to develop a strategy to combat this legacy habit and chop it off right from the roots. Following are some of the measures that can be taken to deal with this:

1. Analyze your core beliefs and evaluate where they actually stem from.
2. Introduce a new way of thinking, so that the old ways could be discarded.
3. Asking questions and rationalizing situations can also give you deeper understanding of your own business.
4. Being prepared to allow new ideas to come in and implementing on them.
5. Encouraging employees to think like a child and introducing interesting ideas to keep them motivated.
6. Working in accordance with the current trends.
7. Sticking to facts while still holding on to curiosity.

Core beliefs can literally blur out your outlook on life and can have a negative impact on your mindset. These core beliefs largely affect our thinking in today's age as compared to our thinking back in the day. They sometimes instill a sense of negativity and can be incurable to some extent. Thus, thinking like a child is highly advisable and significant in eliminating biased self-talk, so that we can have a positive outlook on life. We will study further about this in the next chapter.

Chapter 3

Why Thinking Like A Child Can Be A Positive Outlook on Life?

In a world that is constantly trying to manipulate us and slowly transform our mindsets, we find little room for our own thoughts to come out. We fail to do things that are solely the product of our own imagination and creativity. The core beliefs that we set up like pillars in our life tend to act as the foundation for every decision we make. We tend to over analyze, over think and over obsess over things that bring negativity. The child-like creativity, as well as the positivity, vanishes.

Core beliefs, which are basically cognitive content infused into our brains, may look something like *"I can't achieve this," "the business may result in losses"* or other things that create a negative outlook on life. This is called self-talk, which we discussed in the previous chapter. It combines your unconscious biases and beliefs with the conscious thoughts that influence your behavior every step of the way, often bringing negative connotations with them.

This negativity can be dispelled with the *"thinking like a child"* principle. It can transform your outlook on life and infuse positivity. Thinking like a child makes you go back to the days when you did think and analyze, but that process was unaffected by any kind of adult bias. You thought without keeping the issue within the frame of what has been taught to you already. You always imagined the positive outcomes to everything regardless of others' opinions, which is why curiosity was the most prominent personality trait in you.

Curiosity is filled with positivity. A negative mind can never be curious as it will always be filled with fear and doubt. This negativity can withhold you from achieving great things in life. Now, negativity does not just appear in our lives out of nowhere. It is slowly and gradually engraved into the perceptions and workings of our mind through societal influences. Let us look at how negativity has been planted inside our heads as we have grown older.

The Negativity Planted By the World

When we were born, we were unaware of the ways of this world. We had no idea what race, religion, politics and culture were. We were free from any and all forms of moral or societal influences. This freedom made us think out of the box – identify the unique things around us and look at problems differently, all with the aim to learn. We were creative and imaginative; there was no place for self-doubt, fear or negativity. Gradually, the preconceived beliefs made way into our minds and we began to think in accordance with them. Society, religion, culture, and politics conditioned our minds to think in relation to them regardless of whether they had a role to play or not. Anything that was not in accordance with what the world taught us was considered to be foolish. Even though all this was supposedly introduced to us for our own benefit, so we could be better acquainted with the world's mechanisms, it eventually transformed us into mechanical creatures who have lost their originality, and do only what have been embedded into them. There are several ways in which our brains are influenced from the moment we are born.

Family/Peers: As we learned earlier, family is the primary institution where we learn to do the most basic activities like walking, eating, and talking. It is difficult to imagine yourself not to be influenced by it. For example, a child brought up in a family whose members usually talk in their native language is likely to develop the same accent as he grows up. His choice of words, the taste in food that he may develop, the way he dresses up, among many other traits, will all be similar to the other family members. This is because, growing up, they have an example set before them. If the parents call something good, they consider it to be desirable whereas if the parents will call something bad, they will consider it to be detestable. It is no surprise then that it is the most influential method of incorporating a level of positivity and negativity in us. A child growing up in a family with divorced parents or domestic violence is more likely to have a negative outlook in his personal relationships and decisions.

Similarly, peers are a very important part of your life. Peer pressure can mold your thoughts and outlook on life. Negative impact from peers can have an impact on your thoughts for the rest of your life. For example, being bullied by friends or being encouraged by them to try certain harmful things may have a negative impact on you in the long run.

Education: There is not a shadow of doubt that education is necessary and expands your knowledge regarding things. However, it also gives a systematic direction to your thoughts, which can prevent you from thinking in a different perspective. Education values logic, which could instill a sense of negativity in you. It may make you think that certain things are not achievable simply because no one has ever tried to achieve them or because they are just perceived to be impossible. Education may put rigid beliefs in our mind regarding science, psychology or economics. Such subjects include principles that have been backed up by evidence. However, there are other hypothetical theories that are being taught that might not be entirely true. They have just been passed down to us like a legacy, which we are imparting onto the younger generations without any questions. Students are forced to study them and believe them.

Media: The world is driven by media and technology. Everything that is shown on TV or social media is considered to be the ideal way of doing things. Even though media is good in terms of entertainment and spreading awareness about issues, it can subconsciously influence the core beliefs that may make us negative. Media can keep us focused on what is going on around the world, and we rely on that information because we are unable to do our own research. For example, crime on TV can make us develop fear and we may become anxious when we step out of the house. Social media can make us superficial and materialistic because of the constant exhibition of glamorous lifestyles online. People may tend to feel depressed when they discover that other people are doing better than them. These things can have a negative impact on masses, and with its constant advancement, it is difficult to mitigate its effects.

Cultural Norms: Cultural norms are a part of every society and they vary accordingly. However, some of these norms may support ideas that create a negative environment. For example, stereotyping and generalizing can hinder people from leading their lives freely. In some cultures, racism may be practiced, or gender discrimination may take place. It is a result of what the culture promotes and how they treat their people. For instance, some cultures may still consider women to be inferior to men despite the fact that in our current global state, women are doing impeccably in whichever field they are in. Also, people with dark skin may still be looked upon with contempt while in other cultures, dark-skinned people may be considered as beautiful. Such things can lower people's self-esteem and not only create a negative mindset in the victim's mind, but also in the minds of the people practicing them. Children may grow up having the same negative beliefs and values, which may have severe impacts on their personalities, as well as of others.

Politics/Religion: These are highly influential mediums to build our core beliefs. Although, political and religious beliefs are not entirely negative, they can fill our minds with biases. This is because they can trigger negative thoughts towards people whose religious and political beliefs are different from ours. These beliefs may be a part of our lives because they have been taught to us and are not a result of our own choosing.

Effects of Negativity

While negativity may seem like a word that is not too harmful, the effects of it can be devastating on a personal level. Following are the effects that negativity can have on your life:

1. **Negativity May Affect You Mentally.**

   Negativity planted in our brains can affect our mental health. It can result in lowered self-esteem, as well as other psychological issues such as depression and anxiety. Self-talk can demolish your confidence and may make it difficult for you to cope with every day challenges of stress.

2. **Negativity May Affect You Physically.**

   Negativity works under the surface, deep within your mind, but it has visible effects on your physical health. You can develop diseases and severe health problems due to the negativity that was ingrained into you many years ago. This negativity may largely be a consequence of unhealthy relationships in the family or negative things spoken to you by your peers.

3. Negativity May Harm Others.

As much as negativity can affect you, it can also affect the people around you. Negativity in your mind can cause you to become angry, selfish, and violent, which may make other people suffer. It can have harmful effects on your family, peers, and anyone in your environment. Discriminatory beliefs and values can make you judgmental and hateful towards others, which may cause further negativity in their life.

4. Negativity May Have a Harmful Impact on Your Future.

It can make you a hopeless person. You may become someone who self-doubts and has fears. This is going to stop you from giving your best in whatever you do. You may not even try a lot of things out of the fear of failure. This can make it difficult for you to hope for a better future, and you may just develop anxiety by obsessing over tomorrow. Negativity can not only ruin your present, but it can ruin your future due to you not taking any risks and positive decisions.

5. Negativity May Cause Problems in Your Work/Business.

A business requires a high-level of positivity to ensure that the leader and the employees both are willing to work together in the long run. Positive thinking results in positive outcomes. Similarly, negative thinking can easily result in negative outcomes. For example, if a person is already anticipating a loss in his business, it is likely that he will not generate considerable profit because of his negative thinking.

Negativity Eradicated by Thinking like A Child

Negativity can only be eradicated by adopting a principle that would create positivity in us. Therefore, the only way to do this is by *"thinking like a child."* It can enable us to do things that children naturally do. They push limits and explore beyond their abilities. As a child, there is no sign of negativity in our lives because we think without being influenced by the above-mentioned sources of negativity. We only do what we think is right and fascinates us. A child has no sense of fear or doubt because their only focus is on what they want to do.

Thinking like a child eliminates all possibilities of complying with what media, education, religion or culture says. Although, the point is not to completely ignore these values, as they cannot be overlooked if we want to survive in society, it is to just embrace the self-esteem building and creativity infusing qualities that can only enter into our lives if you choose to think like a child. You become healthier in physical and mental terms, and you become receptive to new ideas. You become more constructive and productive as the external invaders that pollute your thoughts are washed away, giving you a clearer perspective.

A Positive Outlook on Life

Therefore, thinking like a child helps you have a more positive outlook on life and a clearer perception of things. Similar to a child's mind, you become less concerned with the negativity that is going on around you and your only concern remains to explore and to learn. This positive outlook can improve your life in many ways, even when it comes to running a business.

1. **Creativity and Imagination:**

   Having a positive outlook on life can make you more creative. You begin to think of new ways in which you can express your ideas and thoughts. You use your imagination to the fullest because just like a child, you become unafraid of any possible negative repercussions. You think in an inventive way and use your talents to build and construct to use your capabilities to the fullest.

2. **More Possibilities:**

   It can increase your possibilities of accomplishing goals that may otherwise seem unattainable. Negativity can set barriers in your head as you may tend to think that you are not capable enough.

However, positivity erases all those barriers and you begin to think of obtaining whatever it is that you want.

3. Ignoring the Criticism:

A child knows nothing about criticism. He is unaffected by what people would call him or how his failures will turn people against him. His only focus is to try new things and make new discoveries. Therefore, this positivity enables you to ignore all negative comments that may come from family, peers and society.

4. New Experiences:

This positive outlook on life will encourage you to make new experiences. You will develop an eagerness to learn from others and will not think too highly of yourself. A child is humble and accepting of new ideas. Similarly, you will always be ready to let new ideas influence you and teach you.

Impact of This Positivity on Your Business

The positive outlook promoted by child-like thinking can have positive effects on your business as well. The child-like innocence can be strangely great for it because this kind of thought-process is flexible and not limited to any rules or regulations. You can easily make your business more innovative. Innovation holds a lot of value in the current business world. Old conventions of business, as well as entire industries like advertising and marketing, have been discarded, with new ways being introduced daily.

Therefore, it is essential to incorporate a positive mindset to achieve positive results, not just in your life but also in your business.

A positive outlook on life can help you identify something unique in everything you do. Unlike other businesses, you can adopt to new strategies and plans so that your company may stand out in the market. This will attract new clients and will open new doors for opportunities. Your business will thrive and prosper like never before. Thinking like a child creates the willingness to learn and educate yourself. Consequently, you will learn more and will be better educated with what is going on in the market. You will learn to accept the changes and fluctuations in prices, as well as how to take risks and make decisions that will benefit your overall outcome in the future. Moreover, this positivity will give you the motivation you need to discover uncharted areas. You will be ready to make new discoveries. This child-like innocence will also allow you to identify opportunities and be more hopeful.

In a nutshell, thinking like a child can have a positive outlook on your life, your business and the people around you. While core beliefs and self-talk can have a negative impact, this kind of thinking can rectify that and prove to be life-changing in many advantageous ways. In the next chapter, we will learn more about the impact of self-talk and see some of its examples.

Chapter 4

Real World Examples of Self-Talk Impacts

Self-talk can have damaging effects on your personal life and your business. This makes it vital for aspiring entrepreneurs like you, to manage your self-talk effectively. Your actions and who you are as a person is largely dependent on what you think about. Therefore, you need to take charge of your thoughts if you want to control its impact on your business as well. Oftentimes, you may find yourself setting up the business, making judgments about the profits, and the impact of it on the economy and consumers. This may cause you to think that the chances of success in your business are quite limited. You may tend to back off and withdraw yourself from an opportunity by just being influenced by the self-talk and assumptions going on around you.

In this chapter, we will look at some real-world examples of my experiences with self-talk. It would give you an idea of how self-talk can be destructive and obstructive primarily when it comes to business, and how it can one overcome it with mindfulness and unreliability on what the world feeds into our minds. This will further deepen our understanding on thinking like a child, and its immense importance even after years of obtaining experience and knowledge. Thinking like a child defies all perceptions that develop a sense of negativity in us and enables us to look at the brighter side of the situation.

We always have self-talk involved in whatever decisions we are about to make whether it is personal or related to business. We start making assumptions and talk about what we truly believe are the possibilities of a certain thing. Therefore, here are a bunch of stories that really taught me a lesson about self-talk, and I hope you could benefit from it too.

Self-Talk Hinders Through Questioning

The first story includes three of my fraternity brothers and myself. On Christmas break, we travelled to Acapulco, Mexico for a surfing trip. We drove from Gainesville, Florida and it was a long trek. We were typical college students with not a lot of money in the pocket so when we got to Acapulco, we decided to stay at a place which would be inexpensive for us.

We were of the opinion that the most inexpensive place one could go to would probably be a trailer park or a camping site. Therefore, we went to the Balboa trailer park. There we rented a concrete slab for the night and we would take our sleeping bags to go and sleep out in the wild, under the stars. Because of renting the concrete slab, we were able to save money. So, we were there for 3 to 4 days surfing and having a good time. On the last day however, one of the guys we were travelling with fell sick as a result of food poisoning.

We had eaten out earlier that night. Out of the sickness and agitation, he finally said, *"I don't really care how much it costs but I'm not sleeping on the concrete out under the stars again. I'm just going to pay the extra money and get a room at this place."*

The Balboa place had rooms too. Anyway, we all sat there self-talking and telling him, *"Well, it's going to be a lot of money."*

He said, *"I do not care."*

He went inside to get a room for himself. He got a room and asked about the cost of it. Here is where self-talk impacted us. We had never asked how much the room cost. To our astonishment, the room was about 40% cheaper than the concrete slab. We had been thinking this way because it was camping, but it came out to be cheaper. Our self-talk had made us sleep three nights out in the elements on hard concrete when for less money we could have easily got a nice air-conditioned room in Acapulco, Mexico.

Staying Within the Boundaries

Another self-talk story dates back to when I was little. By that time, I had only two brothers as the third one was not born. We were almost about the same age; 12-year-olds. I was the oldest among them then I had a second brother who was a year behind me and then another brother who was a year behind him. Every year, my grandparents would ask us to give them a Christmas list of our wants.

I remember sitting around the table, all wanting bicycles and talking to ourselves. My first brother said that he was going to put down a 10-speed bicycle on the list.

When the youngest brother and I heard this, we said, *"Are you crazy? They are never going to spend the money on a 10 speed."*

With this thought in mind, I put down a 5-speed bicycle because it seemed much more reasonable and I figured that my grandparents would get me a 5-speed bicycle with the money. The youngest brother put down a 3-speed bicycle. This is how we convinced ourselves. My brother who asked for a 10 speed was quite convinced he had had asked for the right thing and exactly what he wanted. My other brother and I were much smarter than him, so I put down 5 speed because I knew that had to be clearly within the price range and he put down 3 speed, thinking that the other two of us were crazy.

So, on Christmas morning, we went to our grandparents for the presents. My grandfather always had a unique way for our gifts. This time there was an envelope on the Christmas tree for each of us. We opened the envelope and it said go to the back door, and you will find string with your names on it. So, we went back and each of us found a string. My grandfather was always fond of such crazy surprises. We followed the strings that kind of wound around the backyard and around the plants.

As we were young to figure out anything with cleverness, we just followed the string as we were instructed. We had that same child-like curiosity and we were ready to explore what lay in store for us. I was convinced that I was smarter than my other brothers were, but thoughts kept coming into my mind.

I thought maybe there were no bikes at all and our grandparents had bought something according to their own wish or maybe we all were going to get 3 speed bikes if possible. However, we followed the strings and they led to the garage door. We opened the door and there stood three bicycles. There was a 10 speed, a 5 speed and 3 speed bike. Our self-talk had allowed us to get exactly what we convinced ourselves would be within the feasibility of giving. If we all had asked for what we really wanted, we would have had three 10 speed bikes sitting there. That day we received a really big lesson that we shouldn't have self-talk ourselves too much as we ended up with exactly what we believed, not what we really wanted to end up with. Furthermore, it proved how two of us ended up not getting what we really wanted, and my other brother was the most successful by not believing our self-talk.

Facts vs. Opinions

One more example is related to a business that I ran. It was a laser hair removal business so, we catered in the women industry. However, around 2008 to 2007, the economy was starting to fall apart. In the wake of this, all my teams and the people in the industry began to self-talk about how devastating this was going to be for the business and how the economy was going to slow it down. Unemployment was plus 10% and people would, simply not have the money to make this purchase. At this point, I had pretty well adopted the kind of vetting self-talk for myself.

Back in the 60s, Daniel Patrick Moynihan coined a phrase *"Everyone is entitled to his own opinion, but they are not entitled to their own facts."* The fact of the matter is that due to the presence of competition in the whole industry, people were freaking out about the economy. The unemployment had increased, there was a housing crisis, and people were losing jobs.

As a result of all this, the question was who was going to buy goods and services. The customer base of our company was 25 to 40-year-old females. According to what the facts stated, not the opinions, due to the height of the recession the unemployment rate for our age segment for female never increase above four and a half percent. It was clearly statistical full employment. Everybody that could be our customer had a job. The average household income of our customer was $37,000. They were not rich people by any stretch. So, they not only did they have a job, but everybody was within the economic framework of what our business was built around.

As our team understood the facts versus what dangers the economy displayed or how everybody was sharing how bad it was, we learned to deal with only the important facts. We cut the self-talk and our company continued to be mega successful. The company continued its success and that led to the successful sale of the company for $175 million a few years later. This was living proof for all of us that even in a recession, the business could be highly successful, if only one learns to eliminate the self-talk. During recession, it would have been easy to fall into that pitfall of self-talk and believe in the failing economy, which was not a relevant factor applicable to our specific customer base. Instead, our business got better as we paid more attention towards facts versus opinions.

Searching For Possibilities

I had a tire company and I needed to buy new trucks. At this time, I had not learned how to eliminate self-talk and believing in what can happen without exhausting all possibilities. So, we were looking at buying new trucks and we were kind of a turnaround company. Everybody was convinced that we would not get the trucks as we did not have good credit. We then started to work on getting financing with our bank. The bank kept coming up with more things they needed to know in order to get the deal done. The list and hassles kept impacting getting the deal done. More and more list of things that were needed to be done, and all the while they failed to make a decision. The vice president of the commercial department said, *"Dean, we're going to get this done, just be patient."*

Finally, the trucks arrived at the dealership and were ready for us to get them. Now, I wanted the trucks to be 100% financed with no money down, because we were adding equipment in it, too. This is where self-talk came in. The bank finally came back and said this was impossible to do. So, I went to the truck dealership and told them what financing I needed and how I wanted it structured. They looked at me and said *"it shouldn't be a problem at all"*.

Now again, had I just taken the word of everybody around me and all the self-talk going on about how it was not possible, this would not have been possible. I went and said exactly what I wanted, and they agreed to sell me five trucks. Well, here's the crazy part of the story. I not only got the trucks financed and signed all the paper work, I in fact got it at a better rate than my bank had promised me. In reality, my bank couldn't get the deal done. Everybody was telling me skeptically that I would not be able to get it done.

This would have been easy for me to believe and throw in the towel like so many people do. Anyway, when I went to sign the paperwork at the truck dealership to get the five trucks, they had the deal at a better intertest rate than I was being told at my bank and it was exactly what I wanted in terms and everything else.

Surprisingly, the paper work printed out for me to sign and it was from my actual bank. My bank was working through the car dealership. The dealership got us a better interest rate and 100% financed, exactly what I wanted. This became possible by refusing to believe the deal couldn't get done and having others use their facts and resources to help make it happen.

That was a real-world example where it would have been easier to be discouraged that 100% financing was impossible according to what the people said. Moreover, we learn that if you explore and challenge what the possibilities are, you can achieve the seemingly impossible.

Asking Questions like A Child

The last story is really a strong example of thinking like a child.

I had a manufacture that sold us products. I would fly a couple of times a year to visit with my major supplier's CEO. I did this to build relationships. Most people never take trips to visit their vendors on their turf. I learned years earlier how valuable this technique was in getting support I might need from them.

So, I flew to meet the CEO of the company. I had been up to see them two or three different times. I've found that as the customer most companies never go to see their vendors or the head of the company on their turf.

On about my third visit, the particular person asked me, *"What can I do to help your company grow?"* This was perfect timing because we had started to grow and we needed capital and I said, *"I would like one and a half million dollars interest free for three years."*

He looked at me and he started laughing and said, *"that's impossible, we can't do that."*

I said, *"But you asked me what I needed, and that's what I need? Why don't you think about it and instead of telling what you can't do, let me know what you can do. "*

Then I got on an airplane and flew back to Tampa.

A day and a half or two days later, this particular CEO of the company called me up and said, *"Dean, we did a lot of thinking about it and we're going to give you exactly what you wanted."* They gave me 1 and half million dollars interest free for three years, which allowed us to grow and create a successful company with capital at no charge. We bought our products from them and it helped their company as well. Again, can you imagine if I had gone through self-talk and said that there are no possibilities because everybody said nobody would ever do that and you're crazy, nobody would ever give you an interest free loan for three years, it's impossible. We would've never gotten the money and probably never had the successes we had as a company by virtue of gaining this important capital source.

Similarly, there are going to be a lot of situations where people are going to try and tell you what can't happen. But think again with the same innocence of a child. A child would not give up asking. They will keep asking you till you almost break down and give in. You can apply the same theory to business situations. When you refuse to listen to self-talk, you will generally find very good circumstances or outcomes by not assuming and listening to people. Thinking like a child removes assumptions and makes you believe that everything is possible.

The Impact of Thinking like A Child in a World Driven by Self-Talk

With so many examples I have experienced in my personal and business life, you can see how the constant work of self-talk can limit the possibilities in our lives. In some cases, we may not even be aware of how it is influencing us. However, with what I learned from the incidence of truck dealership and with the other myriads of examples of prominent figures in the world of business or creativity, you will find how self-talk is in fact eradicated by thinking like a child.

Vice president of Lazzara Yachts Company, self-described as *"Gen neXt entrepreneur,"* Rich Lazzara, stated in a blog he recently published; *"To be a successful entrepreneur, think like a child. The biggest obstacle to creative ideas is fear of failure, he says, pointing to the self-defeating statements we often repeat in our heads; 'I'm not creative.' or 'I can't think of anything.' You need to forget that attitude and allow yourself to open up to failure. When you sit down to create an idea, go into it with zero inhibition."* According to him, another way to deal with this is to refuse to be limited by factors such as time and money. He says. *"As you are preparing to come up with your ideas, it is important that you not set restrictions on yourself. Allow yourself to think completely free."*

Charlie O'Donnell also shared his experience of starting a startup by thinking like a child. He said that entrepreneurs should not spend time chasing venture capital at the start of the business. But instead their only focus should be on the business' growth, and the venture capital will come to them. He also spoke about this at the NJ Tech Meetup. *"Start a company. Build it. Grow it. And then one day when everything is starting to take off, you magically learn about this thing called venture capital which you've never heard about before. You don't start a company with your first major milestone being to close venture funding. You build something awesome and then you might be ready for VC, but you should never raise capital in hopes of building something awesome."*

Despite the presence of so many contemporary examples, the world's most intelligent man Einstein also believed in the importance of thinking like a child. As a child, he was very curious which stayed with him as he grew old. When he was about 5 years old, he was sick in bed one day and his father brought him a compass. He examined the mysteriousness of the compass and was fascinated. This was the first time his intellect was stirred, and this motivated him for the rest of his life. *"I can still remember—or at least I believe I can remember—that this experience made a deep and lasting impression on me."* he wrote.

This encouraged Einstein to spend his life working on field theories. Starting from such a young age, who knew that Einstein would grow up to be attracted to mysteries of science, life, and the universe? He later said to a friend in a letter; *"People like you and me never grow old. We never cease to stand like curious children before the great mystery into which we were born."*

Self-talk is the only factor that can limit our minds to the conventional beliefs. Like the life of great people, I have referenced, it also bears witness, thinking like a child gives us hope in a world that is so occupied in worries that it fails to question the most basic things. Consequently, they lose the desire to go beyond possibilities. I, too experienced self-talk at numerous times in life but I hope these real-world self-talk impacts would enlighten you to break the chains of self-talk and embrace a more principled approach of thinking like a child.

Chapter 5

Developing Child-Like

Thinking In Your Business

Thinking like a child cultivates innovation and creativity which are the key drivers of business expansion and growth. In a world that no longer regards the old, prosaic business and marketing strategies as desirable, child-like thinking enables your concepts and ideas to stand out as unique and original. It serves you with the opportunity to forsake the ordinary ways that the world has adapted to and display your own imagination without the boundaries of the preset rules and regulations. Incorporating this idea and making it the foundation of your business can therefore lead to a successful business. Entrepreneurs must draw inspiration from children because of their boundless curiosity which allows them to ask questions, think out of the box, be unaffected by preconceived notions and core beliefs. These are highly beneficial to practice good leadership, maintain a colorful and innovative workplace culture and value the personal and mental growth of your employees by eliminating all negativity that reduce the creative output of the business.

It might be astonishing to you that there are still businesses that remotely consider innovation to be a key asset for their business and consider child-like thinking to be a mere foolish approach. This is because they misunderstand the whole concept of "Thinking like a child" and how developing this thought process in your business can help you achieve success. They are reluctant to leave behind their previous ways and be open to new ideas and concepts. It's a tragic fact because it can make you stick around the same conventional strategies and ideas when you are capable of doing and thereby achieving so much more. There are great business innovators who have embraced "child-like thinking" which has made them accomplish success. Steve Jobs, Elon Musk, Larry Page and Reif Hoffman are some prominent examples of entrepreneurs who have infused their child-like thoughts into their businesses and have made a place for themselves in the world of innovation. Thus, in this chapter, you will learn about the process of developing this child-like mindset and how you can use it for a greater purpose. You will learn some important tools that will help you develop this thinking process within your company. People are still ignorant about the wonders that this type of thinking can do but I encourage you to unleash your child-like abilities and then sit back and watch how your business flourishes.

The Importance of Questioning

One of the main attributes of children especially at the early stages of cognitive development is that they are so inquisitive that they ask tons of questions. In addition to those questions are the follow-on questions which may be raised if they fail to understand or agree with what you have shared with them. They will ask why, how and express the curiosity that may drive you crazy. You may wonder when they will ever stop asking questions. As your child grows up, that curiosity diminishes, and they don't ask as many questions as they did before. However, this is the kind of approach to life that we need in our companies. "Asking Questions" is not a sign of ignorance, foolishness or obnoxious behavior. Instead it is a sign of curiosity and the desire to learn more about something. Therefore, questioning and curiosity must be encouraged in your workplace to promote learning, creativity and innovation. The more questions you ask, the more your mindset will expand. Your ideas will turn more creative as you view things from a distinct perspective just like children do. So, in the case of developing child-like thinking in your business, you will have to teach yourself and your team to ask questions and to challenge everything including the status quo.

An apt demonstration of this whole approach of asking questions is a TV show named "Colombo." It came on many years ago and is based on a book. This TV show includes the story of a detective who had this crazy ability to ask questions. He constantly asked questions and his biggest kind of technique was when everybody thought was done asking questions, he would basically start walking away and then turn around, asking one more question. That question would usually be one that totally caught everybody off guard. This was his strategy to reach down to the very core essence of the facts and thereby solve the most difficult cases.

Similarly, you must also learn the importance of asking questions. Once you learn how to ask questions, you should teach your team to do the same. This will help them grow on a personal and professional level and you will reap benefits out of it too. One great benefit would be that you will stimulate ideas when your team will ask questions. Asking questions will ignite a spark in their minds and tap the inner ideas that may not be discovered otherwise. Moreover, it will also eliminate some of the self-talk of vagueness. For instance, whenever somebody says something is too expensive, I would generally ask them how much it costs. And then they would reply, "Well, it's just really expensive.' And I would keep asking them the same question to know the reason why they make that statement. It is amazing how quickly someone would come to a conclusion without pondering much about why they consider a certain thing to be expensive. You can stop many possible opportunities by having such a vague statement. However, by questioning you can examine the reasons why something is so expensive and make wise choices accordingly. This is going to be very helpful for you as an entrepreneur as you will think about you can do to be more successful or in some cases what can be done to satisfy customers and how to use your assets and finances is the best way possible.

Asking questions will also help you be familiar with facts and you can use many tools available for that. Once you begin making use of that, you will find them extremely beneficial and you will refrain from making wrong decisions. When I look at the current modern world with internet and technological advancement and literally everything at your disposal, I really wish I had it when I was in my 20s and 30s. I didn't have these when I started my business career and I had to dig out the hard way to gain information regarding facts. But now that you have the internet, you can use the search engine and dig out whatever information you need. You can also get knowledge of national data that is factual and is based on surveys and actual census information. So, when you are very specific with your facts, it really makes a difference in your business. It enables you to eliminate vague terms and a lot of times you may find your own set of blind spots as well, but this will challenge your own mindset and will enlighten you with the factual information. Furthermore, as you teach your team to ask these more pointed questions, you will encourage them to constantly challenge the status quo which will result in breakthroughs and elimination of a lot of your own blind spots. Therefore, you must not cut your teams off by enforcing your own belief system or business policy. Instead, allow them to ask questions just like a kid. This will definitely challenge the authority but that does not mean that you have to rollover or allow your company to be wildly crazy with everybody just doing whatever they want. You still have to keep your eyes and ears open at all times to possibilities which will create opportunities which will thereby make your business more successful.

Creating A Vibrant, Creative And Interactive Culture

Creating a colorful and interactive culture in the business environment is essential in stimulating creativity. Children are always drawn to colors and they actively engage in activities that allow them to use their imagination. This keeps the environment light-hearted and enjoyable, keeping the mind at ease. A similar approach to the workplace environment can also be allowing nap breaks, video games, and other activities. These can create a childlike thinking process and a creative workplace culture. It will promote interactions other than business related conversations and boost the performance and productivity of the employee. It will also bring out hidden talents and interests which can help you understand your employee better and apply those talents to your business in accordance with that. Your employee's imagination and creativity is your power and you have to unleash it in order to thrive.

Practice Appreciation And Celebration

When the business undergoes loss, the entrepreneur and the employee equally suffer the loss. There may meetings and discussions as to what must be done and what resulted in the particular set back. However, when a milestone is achieved, or an employee does well, there is little appreciation shown to them and in some cases, there may not be any feedback for their performance. But these things are the key to boost the employees' productivity. Appreciating and encouraging the team can do wonders as it the source of motivation. In addition, celebrating the success, or an employee's birthday or just work anniversaries can result in a morale boost and be a reminder that they have the company's support as they are likeminded in the pursuit of their goals and seek the overall welfare of the company.

Spend Time Together

Food invitations, get-togethers, picnics and outings are another way to bring people together. Planning out such events can enable you to bring your team in an environment where they can take a break from work related things and stress and just have light-hearted interactions. On such occasions, colleagues can get to know each other and share their personal interests. Laughter is a great way to break the ice and build relationships. Therefore, as the team members come together you will be surprised to see the change in their attitudes towards each other and the company. Their friendliness will create a stronger bond which help in future business ventures.

Encourage Transparency

Business relationships are just like any other relationship. A strong relationship is girded by trust, loyalty and transparency. Having friction and distance between people working together for a shared vision is harmful for the company. This can result in workplace bullying and discouragement. Also, the employees will not be sharing their personal struggles due to this. Thus, transparency is the key if you want to build a stronger bond with your team. As an entrepreneur you have to instill this trust in their hearts so that they can be honest with you and there aren't barriers between you and them.

Be Authentic And Allow Authenticity

Authenticity makes your ideas and concepts more valuable. In an age of innovation and continuous advancement, it is imperative to cultivate authenticity in your workplace culture. As a leader, you have to practice this first to set an example for the people working under your authority. A company that encourages plagiarism and replication shows how backwards they are. On the contrary a company who aims at authentic concepts and promotes originality gains recognition for its uniqueness in the business world.

Allow Your Team To Make Choices And Have A Sense Of Control

To encourage a creative office culture, you have to give flexibility to your team. Allow them to make choices on their own and prioritize their input. This can give them a sense of control and they won't feel restricted. Placing restrictions can only pressurize the employee and reduce the freedom of expression.

Have Fun!

Above all, having fun life's key element. Anything that is done without enjoyment is not going to last very long. Therefore, if you want to sustain and progress the imaginative and creative output of your team, you have to allow them to enjoy the work they are doing. As they say, "all work and no play makes Jack a dull boy." So, will it make your employees dull and will it rust their brains if the aspect of fun is detached from the workplace.

Notice, how the above-mentioned factors are found in the life of children. Ranging from appreciation and celebration, authenticity and transparency to having a certain level of control over things and overall enjoying them is what marks the life of a child. All of these are practiced in school and homes which makes children so creative and lively. As we grow older, these aspects are reduced from our lives. Therefore, it is essential to use these strategies to kindle that same childishness again. Developing the process of thinking like a child starts with you and once you begin to nurture and cultivate it, you will find that there is no better approach to business than the one that we have failed to value and cherish i.e. thinking like a child.

Chapter 6

Becoming The Leader

Without Self-Talk

Societal norms and values, social pressure, past criticisms, and fears combine to form a stream of thoughts that breathe negative self-talk into existence. We begin to internalize a conversation within ourselves that constantly reminds us of our insecurities, failures, and shortcomings. While this may be quite motivating in terms of self-improvement and competing with the challenges in the world of business, it is more harmful than helpful in the long run. It can cause stress, frustration, disappointment, self-hatred, and excessive negativity not just in our relationship with ourselves but also in our surroundings. In short, self-talk can be devastating for you as a leader because it will not only influence your life but will radically impact your team.

Today, if you find yourself engulfed in self-talk, then it is time that you come to the realization that you are your biggest asset. Your talent, skills and intelligence are incredible resources that you hold within. Once, you learn to recognize your own importance and value. Thus, encouraging you to start investing in yourself. This will allow you to cultivate growth and eventually build up a strong, successful team which is your second biggest asset. When you are investing in the biggest asset i.e. yourself, it is important to trust your gut and follow your instincts. Trust in yourself in order to make better and quicker decisions. The late Steve Jobs is a great example for us in this matter. He created Apple after failing multiple times and his struggle inspired him to continue investing in himself to achieve his goals. We need to have the same perseverance and believe in our own self. Therefore, in this chapter, you will learn how to invest in yourself and what you can do to be a strong leader that supports a culture of eliminating self-talk.

Finding A Local CEO Group

The first step you can take to invest in yourself is by trying to find a local CEO group. There are many groups out there where different CEOs and owners of businesses get together, share ideas and bring prosperity. There's a chamber of commerce in the local communities where they have classes, unlike the mixers where you get to meet and greet and try to sell each other. It would be better if you find a group with classes where you can learn, get involved in activities and know your peers. Another thing you can do is, if you're in an industry, you can find five or ten more people preferably 10 to 15 that are in the same field. If they live somewhere around the country and are willing to dedicate the time and money, then you can plan to meet once a year for four or five days and share ideas collectively. You must understand that working in the same space means that you are not competitors and therefore, you can learn and work towards growth and success together. The fun part about getting into this group is that when people start sharing ideas, you will find them quite stimulating but in reality, their ideas are stemming from their own desire to do something. They share what they themselves need to do and this gives you an insight into the different challenges that leaders have to face. As a result, you will learn to share your insecurities and talk about your personal battles which might inspire someone else and motivate them to continue pursuing their goals.

Sharpen Your Axe

The next way to invest in yourself is to work towards improving and grooming yourself. Set aside some time to sharpen your axe. I use this term in reference to the story of the two lumberjacks. There was one lumberjack that never lost the wood chopping contest. People from all over would come to challenge him and they would chop wood for eight hours but at the end of eight hours, the big brawny lumberjack would always beat all the challengers no matter how hard they tried. However, there was this one time that a young man came to town. He did not have the burly physique like others, yet he challenged the lumberjack in the wood chopping competition. The townspeople were almost appalled that this young individual could think that he was capable enough to even stand against this lumberjack who had been the champion forever. And so, they started chopping wood and after 50 minutes, the young man took a break in the first hour and disappeared into a shed. Everybody started snickering that he didn't even have the stamina to chop for an entire hour. But he came back after ten minutes and started chopping away the wood. Again, he continued chopping and at the end of the next 50 minutes, he went back in the shed. Yet again, the village people started criticizing the young man's stamina and mocked at his audacity to challenge the lumberjack. At the end of the eight hours of continuous chopping and breaks after every 50 minutes, the cords of wood were counted, and they found that the young man had chopped and produced more wood than the world champion woodcutter. The people of the village were spellbound and began asking questions about how the young man successfully beat the lumberjack despite taking a break after every hour. The young man explained the reason that enabled him to beat the champion was that he didn't actually take a break to rest. In fact, every time he went to the shed, he sharpened his axe for 10 minutes. After sharpening the axe, he would come inside and get back to chopping the wood.

There is a great lesson to learn through this story. The young man's clever strategy was not to keep chopping but to increase the efficiency of his tool and then use it effectively. He knew that no matter how much time he spent hitting the wood, it would be of no use if his axe was not sharp enough. Similarly, our skills and talents are just like the axe. It is likely that you're busy and you're telling your family how overwhelmed you are because of work but it's imperative to understand that amidst the hard work, you have to make sure that your skills are not getting dull like the axe. You have to invest in your skills and sharpen them so that you do not lose what matters to you most. Set aside time to read books and magazines. I subscribed to 100 plus magazines which invariably include magazines that you would least think would ever be in business or personal life but would basically stimulate a thought that would help you be more successful. Reading can enhance your abilities and expand your mindset. As you read about different topics, you begin to learn various strategies related to business and you receive a clarity in vision. Another method to boost your skills takes some classes at your local university related to code writing perhaps. You may be the CEO of a company and you probably would never write code yourself as you already have code writers. Nevertheless, I encourage you to take a class. It will make you intellectually sharper to ask questions, grow and to dismiss self-talk. So, in case a person is talking to you about a business situation, you can ask questions effectively and make them wonder how you are so well-versed in the knowledge that you are familiar with the lingo. Get more expertise and there's no better place to get it than in your local vote tax or your local schools. Take a class regardless of the time whether it is in the afternoon or the evening, whether it is by visiting or doing it at the ease of your home online. You will never regret losing these hours on gaining knowledge. There are a lot of people like you out there, willing to learn and grow and as you interact with them, your skills will sharpen all the more.

Appreciate Your Team And Make Them Feel Valued

Your team is your second biggest asset and it is essential that you infuse positivity and encouragement in them. Interact with them individually and hold meetings where you can promote team building activities. Encouraging them to interact with each other will eliminate all office politics and friction between people who share the same goals. You can do this by taking people in your company once or twice a week to lunch or breakfast. It could even be one of your laborers. While you are having breakfast, get them comfortable with finding out a little bit about them, what makes them tick, what their goals and dreams are, how they see your company, what would they do if they ran the company for a day, etc. What you find is that when you get them out of the work environment, they can think more creatively because they are not repressing their opinions because of the work environment. When they share their ideas, don't disrespect or ignore them but keep a piece of paper and jot down notes to make them feel a part of the team.

I had an experience when I was working with one of my underground pipe crews as a contractor. I was in the ditch and as I listened to my team, they started telling me about a device that would increase our production by 20 percent. I began to think why we wouldn't have this device. This was a device, a tool for them and our team which our management didn't think they needed. So, I asked them what they thought it would do and they said we think it could increase production 20 percent. At the time on this job we had a million-dollar hydraulic backhoe, probably another five hundred thousand dollars in support equipment to lay this sanitary sewer pipeline. These guys were in the ditch dealing with problems and they knew better about what could be helpful for them and ultimately us. So, I immediately sent one of our guys to a local supply company to bring one of these devices. Believe it or not, this device saved our company hundreds and hundreds of thousands of dollars. The device had always been available, but nobody was listening, and nobody was being specific but once they shared their input, we learned about ways to make work easier. Thus, getting associated with your team one on one does work wonders.

I had another experience when I was with one of my other companies at one of our Atlanta offices. We were having a no-show for appointments challenge across the United States. To solve the problem, we developed a reporting process where we would make a confirmation for the following day. I was sitting in one of our locations and listening while we were having this sophisticated process of confirming the appointments for the following day. We had a computer, so they would hit the confirmation and then our system would report to the corporate office that 100 percent of our patients were confirmed. Sounds bullet proof, doesn't it. I was sitting there that afternoon at the desk as one of the team members was making the confirmation calls. The calls went some like, *"Hi. This is so and so from blah blah blah. our company and I'm just confirming your appointment for tomorrow. Thank you or call us if there's a problem."* And the call would end. So, at the end of the calls, I asked our team how often did talk to a person live and they said that they hardly did. By sitting and watching the work in the business for that day, I found a huge disconnect. The fact is we were showing these high confirmation rates that we were having but they were not a sure that the customers were going to come. So, the next day, I told one of the folks on the front desk to ask patients who came in, *"What is the best way you would like for us to ever confirm you?"* A surprising answer came from almost everybody that came in. If given a choice they would like texted confirmations, mainly because they don't answer the phone with numbers that they didn't recognize. So, we basically received an insight into the customer's personal decisions and an active conversation which seemed less like the automated responses. This is a reminder for you, so every day by working in the business and hearing the dilemmas, you should ask your team more questions and be very specific about them. As we were able to determine that another method of communication would help our customers much more, we implemented it immediately. They enjoyed it better and the no-show rate dropped dramatically.

Don't Make An Excuse That You Don't Have Time

The most common excuse that hinders many people from investing in themselves is that they don't have time. They probably do not have time because they are investing that time in something else which further indicates their priorities. They keep themselves last in the list of important things and therefore, after completing all the tasks of the day, when the time comes when they have to do something for themselves then they put it off. However, you need to understand that you are working in your business and if you are making excuses for yourself then you are slowly walking towards death. Investing in yourself multiplies your capacity to perform skillfully. If you continue to make excuses when it comes to yourself, then eventually you will find that you have drained yourself in all hard work. Therefore, make wise choices when you have to allocate time and make sure you do not compromise investing some time in yourself and the things important to you.

Next, invest in your team. Offer educational help to them and always be willing to listen to them. You might fear that even after all your investments, they will leave someday but the truth is that they will not and even if they do then that is a part of your leadership. As a leader, you must not fret about the future but work in day by day to make the future better. Once you grant your employees opportunities for growth, you will find that they will become loyal to you and the company. Your strong commitment towards them eliminates all self-talk on their behalf and helps them grow in a positive work environment where they feel appreciated and understood. Also, give them hundred percent clarity in their vision and responsibility. When you leave a meeting, make sure that everything that was discussed has specific actions in specific terms and that there is set deadlines or set expectations. This will ensure that the employees are working hard and are managing their time correctly.

Thus, before you invest in anything else, invest in your biggest assets i.e. yourself and your team. Learn, grow and explore. Read books and gain knowledge about different perspectives on various subjects. Try to actively read and learn through reading. You can also use this to gain an insight over trends, which can give you an edge. Overall, unleash your curiosity and invest in it. Life is about progressing and as you develop a habit of learning, you will find yourself better than before.

Chapter 7

The Vault Of Stories

That Will Help You As A Leader

"The future is not some place we are going, but one we are creating. The paths are not to be found but made. And the activity of making them changes both the maker and the destination."

-John H. Schaar

Every one of us at some point in life had been a firm believer in fate. Despite striving really hard at accomplishing our goals, we have in the end surrendered like a convict being served a life sentence. We have aligned our thoughts in such a way that we seldom reflect on the fact that our circumstances are in reality the product of our actions and imaginations and not a stroke of luck or a predestined ending to a story. We fail to comprehend that between the beginning of the race and the finish line, there is every step that you have to take to reach there. There is a sequence, an order that must be created to reach the desired goal that we are no longer willing to accept. We forsake the *"in betweens"* and run towards the end.

While there are numerous factors contributing to this, the major reasons behind this is the existence of inevitable challenges. These challenges are like speed bumps on the road which are absolutely unavoidable and slow us down and we wish to avoid them so that we do not have to encounter these struggles. They wear us down and we wish to skip the middle part. These challenges include criticisms, setbacks, our own inabilities to deal with situations, fears that crop up along the road that we have to jump over and our own self-talk which works its way up in our minds as excuses to work towards our goal. These self-talks which is somewhat an amalgamation of all the aforementioned negative factors, not only confines you to a limited space of ideas, notions and opinions but it also tends to divert your mind to foreknowledge. These thoughts cannot necessarily be all positive, as your mind usually directs you towards anticipating failure in case you have witnessed it in the past. You mind whispers lies to you that you cannot carry on in your journey towards success. Therefore, child-like thinking stands as an essential for eliminating self-talk. As a child, we never once thought of the possibility of failure. When we started running, we were focused on each step at a time and we could never think of giving up. When we drew a painting, we never gave up beforehand in the fear of not being able to paint well. In fact, when we did, we enjoy every stroke and freely used colors to reflect our imagination onto paper.

This is what the mindset of a successful, purpose-driven leader looks like. He is ready to take the leap of faith, regardless of what comes his way.

He faces challenges head on and strongly believes that the path he is treading on, is not going to appear unless he takes a step on his own. He does not believe in the negativity that pollutes his mind but with a child-like faith, he creates his future.

Therefore, as we draw near to the end of our journey of learning about the elimination of self-talk, it would be vital to look at the numerous examples of people in the business world who have embraced the same manner of living. They have achieved heights of success because of their refusal to go back or to accept what society has been telling them. There is a plethora of success stories that need to be heard so that you may understand that what you are going through is not new. All success leaders have walked down the same road. Thus, as you read, reflect upon what we have studied so far and learn from these real-life stories of leaders. Furthermore, think about how they reached the ultimate goal and apply those strategies to your personal life. Your story matters, too–the beginning, the middle, and the end.

Examples Of Leaders

As an entrepreneur, you have to face numerous challenges and failures. There may be times when you are torn down by setbacks and while you find zero motivation in your surroundings, you may at the same time be victimized by your own self-talk. In such situations, it is essential to take a glance at the life of other entrepreneurs. Looking at other people's experiences and their entire journey can be very empowering in times of demotivation. Be acquainted with their strategies and how they tackled every problem. Moreover, how they embraced creativity and innovation, and used childlike ways to pave their own pathway to triumph.

Berkshire Hathaway CEO Warren Buffett is a self-made billionaire who started his first business at the age of five. Not just that, but he purchased his first stock when he was eleven-years-old and now he is grown up to be one of world's most successful business investors who is worth over $90 billion. He became one of the richest and most influential people on the globe. While we can only see what he later came to be, there is a long journey that he spent that finally led him to this place. His upbringing played a massive part as it gave him the ambition and creativity that helped him to be the most successful investor.

As a kid, he spent most of his time reading books and his love for reading helped him become a billionaire. Growing up, his favorite book was *"One Thousand Ways to Make $1000"* which inspired him to pursue his entrepreneurial goals. He also suggested reading *"The Intelligent Investor"* the book that led him to succeed. Basically, his desire to be successful was triggered by his love for books when he was a child.

Similarly, Elon Musk the CEO and CTO of SpaceX, chief product architect of Tesla Motors, the co-founder of PayPal, and chairman of SolarCity, has invested in a lot of projects to transform our lives and making it better. He is an inventor, engineer, and innovative entrepreneur who ranks second among the entrepreneurs in the Silicon Valley.

This trending CEO may be the owner of these creative projects, but his creativity flows from his child-like personality. Even at this age, he loves playing video games like bioshock and fallout. Video games make your mind sharper and enhances your ability to think. This is how it impacted Elon Musk's mind.

These may be very small reasons, but they are fuel for creativity for successful leaders. Entrepreneurs like Elon Musk and Warren Buffet do not have a very complicated strategy, but they try to embrace the simplest things in life and use them for the achievement of their goals. These stories are great way to reflect on your own life and understand what boosts your creativity. You may be looking for a great way to carry out your business calling but the answer is in your simple child-like habits.

Let go of the negative, man-made opinions and go back to that child-like state of mind. Be like these successful men and draw your inspiration from things that you liked to do as a kid. Embrace the child in you and make a difference.

Just Do It!

Above all, you need to analyze yourself and make the necessary changes. Eliminating self-talk is the key and you have to train your mind systematically. However, for this you need to take the first step. You have to just do it. Stop overthinking and fretting because that is yet another sign that your self-talk is at work. Stop hiding under the leaves of excuses and muster the courage to embark on this journey. Just like surrendering to fate, we have also very actively used excuses to run away from situations. Remember, the favorite excuses that we all have used in school or while growing up? Remember, when you said your dog ate the assignment because you failed to complete it or when you were late so you blamed the traffic? These are very old habits that have become a part of our lives and when we indulge in self-talk, excuses become our number one means of not stepping out to do what we want to do.

Therefore, the solution is to face the challenges and fear and let go of excuses. A fun way to deal with this can be writing the excuses down and see how you still use those excuse now and how you can quit making them. Writing them down will really help you to get of the excuse mode. There are many successful people who have gone through the same phases but what really helped them make a difference was that they left behind their negative mindset, excuses and self-talk and were willing to try over and over again. Yes, it is a constant struggle but all you need to do is to be specific and think like a child. Be focused on the present and remember that what decisions you take today will make your tomorrow. So, believe in yourself and just do it!

So,

Eliminate

The Self Talk,

Think Like A Child

&

JUST DO IT!

Special Thanks to People That Been a Part of My Journey

(in no special order). Sorry If I missed some one

My Dad, My Mom, My Grandmother, My Uncle Doug, My brothers Doug, David & Drew, My 5 sons; Douglas, Dustin, Dennis, David & Rudy Dean, My current wife, Michelle, My former wife, Debbie, Scott Linder Sr, Ray Phillips, Ed Huffman, Browne Gregg, Hub Williams, Rick Williams, Mark Anderson, John Downer,, Joe Miller, Larry Morgan, Richard Garl, Dan Sherman, Mr. Mathis, Joe Skipper, David Anderson, John Riley, Mike Allsopp, Rick Higginbotham, Tommy Stroud, Bud Mott, Lou Wheeler, Joe Permatteo, Dutch, Keith Koenig, Bob Gesemeyer, Jim Murman, Mike Azzarelli, JW Conner Jr. Mark Mitchell, Terry Aidman, Chip Webster, Gordon Tunstall, Robert Blue, Rebecca Smith, Steve Roebuck, Mark Blumenthal, Misty Spencer, Jeff Hills, Paula, Don Bloebaum, Mike Araldi, Doug Ebbers, Gary Green, Kimberly Trinca, Don Roberts, Rick Mikles, Joe Acebal, Joe Katoe, Bill McBride, Alex Sink, Rob Sulzer, Dr Chris Pittman, Dean Sims, Dean Sims, Jr., Erika Sims, Sheriff David Gee, Bing Kearney, Jim Walter, Sonny Spencer, Donald Conner,